A Beginning

MW01154103

LIFE S

WHAT PLANTS NEED

by Mary Lindeen

NORWOODHOUSE PRESS

DEAR CAREGIVER, The *Beginning to Read—Read and Discover Science* books provide young readers the opportunity to learn about scientific concepts while simultaneously building early reading skills. Each title corresponds to three of the key domains within the Next Generation Science Standards (NGSS): physical sciences, life sciences, and earth and space sciences.

The NGSS include standards that are comprised of three dimensions: Cross-cutting Concepts, Science and Engineering Practices, and Disciplinary Core Ideas. The texts within the *Read and Discover Science* series focus primarily upon the Disciplinary Core Ideas and Cross-cutting Concepts—helping readers view their world through a scientific lens. They pique a young reader's curiosity and encourage them to inquire and explore. The Connecting Concepts section at the back of each book offers resources to continue the exploration. The reinforcement activities at the back of the book support Science and Engineering Practices—to understand how scientists investigate phenomena in that world.

These easy-to-read informational texts make the scientific concepts accessible to young readers and prompt them to consider the role of science in their world. On one hand, these titles can develop background knowledge for exploring new topics. Alternately, they can be used to investigate, explain, and expand the findings of one's own inquiry. As you read with your child, encourage her or him to "observe"—taking notice of the images and information to formulate both questions and responses about what, how, and why something is happening.

Above all, the most important part of the reading experience is to have fun and enjoy it!

Sincerely,

Shannon Cannon

Shannon Cannon, Ph.D.
Literacy Consultant

Norwood House Press
For more information about Norwood House Press please visit our website at
www.norwoodhousepress.com or call 866-565-2900.
© 2019 Norwood House Press. Beginning-to-Read™ is a trademark of Norwood House Press.
All rights reserved. No part of this book may be reproduced or utilized in any form or by any
means without written permission from the publisher.

Editor: Judy Kentor Schmauss
Designer: Lindaanne Donohoe

Photo Credits:
All photos by Shutterstock except; iStock Photo, 22

Library of Congress Cataloging-in-Publication Data
Names: Lindeen, Mary, author.
Title: What plants need / by Mary Lindeen.
Description: Chicago, IL : Norwood House Press, [2018] | Series: A beginning
   to read book | Audience: K to Grade 3.
Identifiers: LCCN 2018004475 (print) | LCCN 2018013276 (ebook) | ISBN
   9781684041541 (eBook) | ISBN 9781599538983 (library edition : alk. paper)
Subjects: LCSH: Life (Biology)-Juvenile literature. | Plants-Juvenile
   literature.
Classification: LCC QH325 (ebook) | LCC QH325 .L6947 2018 (print) | DDC
   570-dc23
LC record available at https://lccn.loc.gov/2018004475

Hardcover ISBN: 978-1-59953-898-3   Paperback ISBN: 978-1-68404-145-9

346R-102021
Manufactured in the United States of America in North Mankato, Minnesota.

How are all of these things alike?
They are all living things.

Living things grow.

People grow.

Plants grow, too.

Did You Know?

People are not plants, but as living things both people and plants need many of the same things.

Living things need water.
People need water.

Plants need water, too.

Plants that need a lot
of water grow in
wet places.

But other plants can grow
in dry places.

Living things need warmth.

People need warmth.

Plants need warmth, too.

Plants that need a lot of warmth grow in hot places.

But other plants can
grow in cold places.

Living things need food.

People have to find their food.

Plants can make their own food.

Living things need sunlight.

Sunlight helps grow
the food people eat.

Sunlight helps plants make their own food.

Plants that need a lot of light grow in sunny places.

But other plants can grow
in the shade.

This plant is working hard
to get the light it needs!

Plants can be changed by the places where they grow.

Plants can also make changes to
the places where they grow.

Watch your step!

Look at the plants around you.
How do they get what they need?

What Plants Need

water

warmth

food

sunlight

CONNECTING CONCEPTS

UNDERSTANDING SCIENCE CONCEPTS

To check your child's understanding of the information in this book, recreate the following graphic organizer on a sheet of paper. Help your child complete the organizer by identifying important facts they learned about plants and writing them in the boxes.

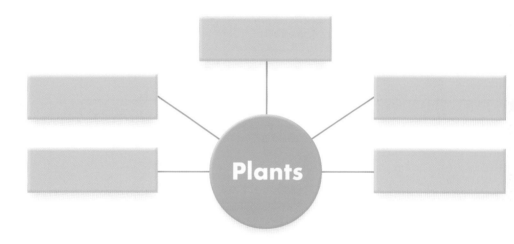

SCIENCE IN THE REAL WORLD

Take a walk in your neighborhood and look for plants that are growing in the sun and in the shade. What do you notice? Then look for plants that are affected by the environment they're growing in. What do you notice about them?

SCIENCE AND ACADEMIC LANGUAGE

Make sure your child understands the meaning of the following words:

alike   liquid   protect   spines   stored

Have him or her use the words in a sentence.

FLUENCY

Help your child practice fluency by using one or more of the following activities:

1. Reread the book to your child at least two times while he or she uses a finger to track each word as it is read.
2. Read a line of the book, then reread it as your child reads along with you.
3. Ask your child to go back through the book and read the words he or she knows.
4. Have your child practice reading the book several times to improve accuracy, rate, and expression.

FOR FURTHER INFORMATION

Books:

Matheson, Christie. *Plant the Tiny Seed*. New York, NY: Greenwillow Books, 2017.

Rattini, Kristin. *Seed to Plant*. Washington, DC: National Geographic Children's Books, 2014.

Williams, Kathryn. *Plants*. Washington, DC: National Geographic Children's Books, 2017.

Websites:

DK Find Out: Plants

https://www.dkfindout.com/us/animals-and-nature/plants/

Growing Chefs!: How Plants Eat

http://www.growingchefs.ca/how-plants-eat

Sid the Science Kid: Growing Plants

http://pbskids.org/video/sid-science-kid/1568868836

Word List

What Plants Need uses the 79 words listed below. *High-frequency words* are those words that are used most often in the English language. They are sometimes referred to as sight words because children need to learn to recognize them automatically when they read. *Content words* are any words specific to a particular topic. Regular practice reading these words will enhance your child's ability to read with greater fluency and comprehension.

High-Frequency Words

a	be	from	look	own	they	work(ing)
all	both	get	make	people	things	you
also	but	have	many	place(s)	this	your
and	by	help(s)	might	same	to	
are	can	how	not	that	too	
around	do	in	of	the	water	
as	eat	is	on	their	what	
at	find	it	other	these	where	

Content Words

alike	cold	hard	living	protect	step	try
animals	dry	hot	lot	shade	stored	warmth
cactus	food	light	need(s)	spines	sunlight	watch
change(d, s)	grow	liquid	plant(s)	stems	sunny	wet

About the Author

Mary Lindeen is a writer, editor, parent, and former elementary school teacher. She has written more than 100 books for children and edited many more. She specializes in early literacy instruction and books for young readers, especially nonfiction.

About the Advisor

Dr. Shannon Cannon is an elementary school teacher in Sacramento, California. She has served as a teacher educator in the School of Education at UC Davis, where she also earned her Ph.D. in Language, Literacy, and Culture. As a member of the clinical faculty, she supervised pre-service teachers and taught elementary methods courses in reading, effective teaching, and teacher action research.